FRACTURED AMERICA

The Many Divisions in the U.S. and How to Fix Them

by Paul Brakke

Author of:

Crime in America,
Fixing the U.S. Criminal Justice System,
The Price of Justice in America,
The Costly U.S. Prison System,
Cops Aren't Such Bad Guys,
and
Dealing with Crime by Illegal Immigrants and the Opioid Crisis

FRACTURED AMERICA

Copyright © 2019 by Paul Brakke

All rights reserved. No part of this book may be used or reproduced by any means, graphic, electronic, or mechanical, including photocopying, recording, taping or by any information storage retrieval system without the written permission of the author except in the case of brief quotations embodied in critical articles and reviews.

ACKNOWLEDGMENTS

I am indebted to Gini Graham Scott for much help in the writing and preparation of this book. Further, I would like to acknowledge the assistance of publicist Jana Collins. My thanks as well to Christin O'Leary for her help with the social media, Alinka Rutkowska for her insights on book launches and promotion, and Gus Sandi for his work on creating the American Leadership Books website. Additionally, I want to thank QuickGraphic99 of 99design for designing the cover for this and my previous book *Crime in America*.

TABLE OF CONTENTS

PREFACE 5
CHAPTER 1: THE RACIAL DIVIDE: ORIGINS 7
   Attitude of Southern Whites toward Blacks 10
   Attitudes of Northern Whites toward Blacks 11
   Attitudes of Blacks toward Whites 12
   Summary 12
CHAPTER 2: THE RACIAL DIVIDE: OUR BLEAK PRESENT 15
   Some Suggested Solutions 19
CHAPTER 3: THE RACIAL DIVIDE: DESEGREGATION AND
AFFIRMATIVE ACTION 23
   The Difficulty of Ending Segregation 24
   Possible Modifications of Affirmative Action 25
   Learning from the Military 26
CHAPTER 4: THE NATIONALITY AND LANGUAGE DIVIDE 29
   The Wall 31
   Alternatives to the Wall 34
CHAPTER 5: GEOGRAPHICAL AND POLITICAL DIVIDES 37
   The North-South Divide 37
   The Divide between the Coasts and Middle America 38
   The Rural-Urban Divide 39
   Some Suggested Solutions 42
CHAPTER 6: OTHER DIVIDES 45
   Ethnic Divides 45
   Generational Divides 45
      How to Understand the Generational Divide 47
      How to Overcome the Generational Divide 49
   Income Inequality 50
      Why Is There So Much Inequality in America? 52
      Some Ways to Fix the Income Inequality Problem 56
   A Threatening Gender Divide 59
CHAPTER 7: WHY WE STILL NEED EACH OTHER 61
   The Increasing Uncivility and Toxicity of the System 62
   Some Ways to Reform the System 64
ABOUT THE AUTHOR 73
OTHER AVAILABLE BOOKS 75
CONTACT US 77

PREFACE

We have to face some grim truths today, or our great nation could easily erupt in flames. The Civil War never really ended. Blacks and whites never really succeeded in mending fences. The North-South divide continues to this date and is further complicated by the divide involving Hispanics, divides between the Coasts and the Middle America, including the Rust Belt. Another division is between rural and urban America. And today the hostility is greater than ever in the party battles between Republicans and Democrats. In addition to these geopolitical divides, there are generational, financial and even gender divides that threaten the country.

To see all this divisiveness, you might conclude that the US is clearly done for. Yet, all partisans on both sides of these divides are interdependent, and that might allow for a glimmer of hope.

This short book will examine these divides in six chapters which attempt to suggest solutions for each division. A seventh chapter examines ways to reconcile those on each side of those divides.

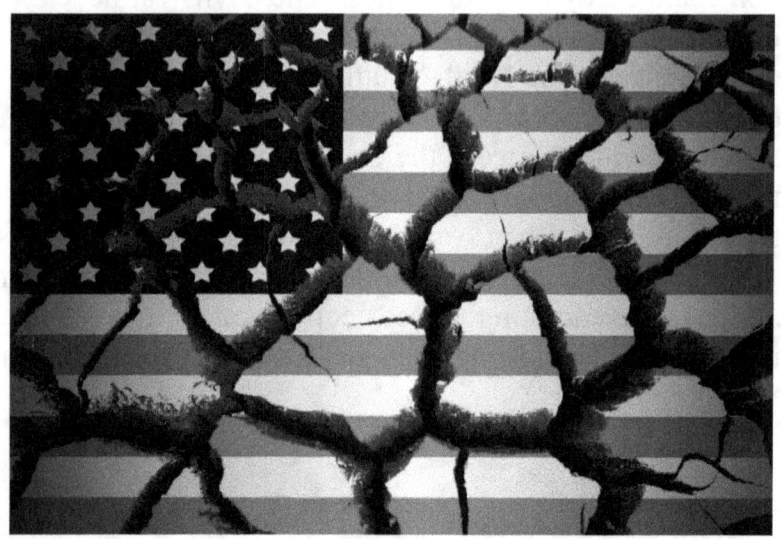

CHAPTER 1: THE RACIAL DIVIDE: ORIGINS

This country was born of slaveholders. The father of the country, George Washington, and many who signed the Declaration of Independence and the Constitution were slaveholders.

Although slaves were treated very badly, they were very valuable. They were considered property -- valuable property. In 1860 each slave cost an average of at least $20,000 in today's dollars. But a lot of wealthy families in the South could afford them: 31% of families in the Confederacy owned slaves, and slaves made up 38% of the South's population.

The entire economy of the South depended on slaves. Their states' rights were being threatened, which led to the inevitable march toward a Civil War less than 100 years after the birth of the country.[1]

The 1860 election of Abraham Lincoln with only 40% of the popular vote in a three person race hastened the onset of the war, and this war was truly horrendous. It accounted for over 600,000 deaths -- as many deaths as all other United States wars combined. And the country still is traumatized by it, particularly the South, as reflected in the support for the

Confederacy and its symbols in many communities throughout the South.

No one expected the Civil War to last as long as it did or claim so many lives. Its opening shots at Fort Sumter in Charleston Harbor in April 1861 had resulted in no loss of life. And the first major battle of the war at Manassas/Bull Run in July 1861 was witnessed by picnicking citizens from Washington 25 miles away. They expected a show with a Union victory which would cause a rapid end to the war. Instead, the Confederates won a bloody victory with hundreds killed and thousands wounded. The next day, Lincoln signed a bill ordering the enlistment of a half million Union troops.

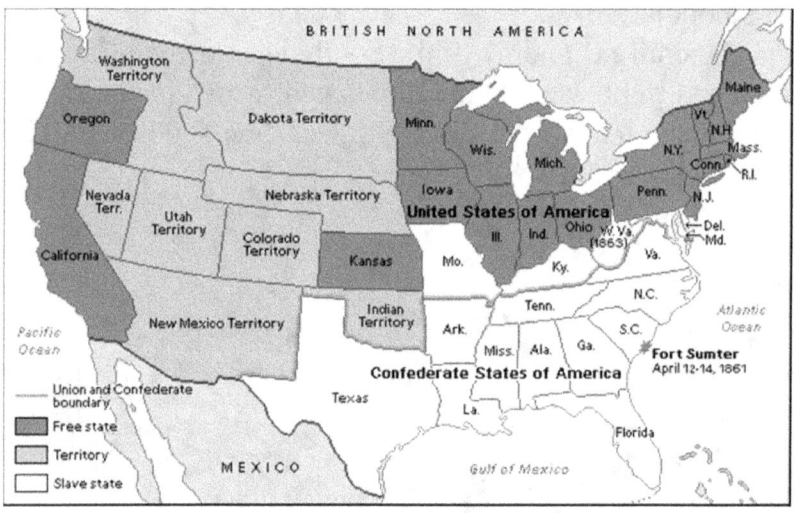

Could the Civil War have been avoided? Probably only by allowing the South to secede, which the North was loath to do. But suppose the South had seceded without challenge from the North. Would slavery still be permitted today? It's not likely, because slavery is not acceptable anywhere anymore. That means that if the South had won and continued to base its economy on the labor of slaves, at some point the South would have had to reform its entire economic system, as well as overcome its resentment about all the freed slaves left living there. It would have made the blacks the scapegoats for all the economic upheavals it experienced, just as it scapegoated them after the Civil War.

Could the Civil War have been terminated earlier? Yes:
- if Confederate General Robert E. Lee had been less reckless in ordering Pickett's suicidal charge against the middle of the Union line at Gettysburg in July 1863 or
- if Confederate General Jubal A. Early's force of over 15,000 troops had managed to blow through a smaller force of only 6000 Union troops at a little known battle at Monocacy Junction on July 9, 1864, they could have captured an undefended Washington, D.C., 46 miles away, or
- if Confederate General John Bell Hood had been less reckless in his defense of Atlanta in July and August of 1864,

then Lincoln would probably have lost the 1864 election, and some sort of truce would have been declared, perhaps even including acceptance of the secession of the Confederacy. Still, at some point the South would have had to give up its slaves, and the same white resentment of blacks would have surfaced.

But the Civil War DID make that resentment far worse. The South was razed by General Sherman's march to the sea. It was completely defeated and had to surrender.

Attitude of Southern Whites toward Blacks

After the war, the South was humiliated and then subjected to profiteering by Northern carpetbaggers. It couldn't even count on its slaves to rebuild. Before the war, the blacks had been considered valuable property, and now that they were rendered free by government fiat, Southerners not only lost the war, but many of them lost their most valuable property.

As a result, the South blamed not only the North but the slaves for its devastation in the aftermath of war. Worse yet, Southerners still had to live with the former slaves. No wonder the whites hated them.

The Southerners feared the blacks, too. After all, they feared that former slaves might want to get their revenge for all those years of mistreatment. Moreover, they fervently believed that white women had to be protected from black males, lest their women be ravished by these former slaves and their progeny.

Given this deep animosity of blacks by the Southerners, for many years the Jim Crow system in the South ensured that blacks were kept in their place. In response, many former slaves migrated to the North in hopes of escaping their plight in the South. Since new job opportunities were concentrated in Northern cities, that's where many of them went.

Even today there are major divisions regarding the Confederate flag and statues of Confederate generals. These are condemned by blacks and liberals as symbols of continued racism and defiantly defended by Southern whites as heroes of their lost struggle and way of life. Southern whites feel the South shall rise again, and indeed in some ways it has. After all, prior to Obama, the previous three Presidents were from the South.

A more constructive attitude exists towards preservation of Civil War battlefields, considered as hallowed ground by those from both the North and South. We should hope that both sides could compromise on the issue by permitting the display of that flag and those statues at those battleground sites without provoking the disdain of blacks. After all, the overwhelming majority of those who died at these battlefields were whites in a conflict that resulted in the abolition of slavery.

Attitudes of Northern Whites toward Blacks

As late as June 1863, after he had issued the Emancipation Proclamation and less than a month before the battle of Gettysburg, the Great Emancipator, President Lincoln, mused about deporting freed slaves to Central or South America.[2] Whites in the North didn't want former slaves coming to compete for their jobs. They had lost a lot of men in the fight to abolish slavery, and the entire nation was financially and emotionally drained. They felt blacks already owed them enough for freeing them. Why couldn't they just stay where they were and be grateful? Since the North had had few slaves, they weren't responsible for slavery. So why should they have to help the Southerners overcome what was their fault in the first place by contributing jobs or money?

Attitudes of Blacks toward Whites

What about black feelings? They had endured slavery for about a hundred years, including in many cases subhuman living conditions and extremely hard labor. They had experienced their families being torn apart and sold, barbaric torture, and even sometimes castration.

Many had remained loyal to their captors, perhaps out of necessity, but most resented their plight and their former masters. The Founding Fathers had written, "All men are created equal," but the blacks knew they didn't count as men to the white Southerners who held the reins of power. To them, the blacks were just beasts of burden, and often they were killed if they were captured after escaping.

Then the Civil War erupted. With the exception of a very few all black units fighting for the North, blacks weren't allowed to fight on either side. They weren't wanted.

Then, suddenly, they were free -- but penniless…and hated and feared by their former captors. They owned no land and were forced into sharecropping, so that now they tended the land for Southern white owners who leased it to them at exorbitant fees. They were free and their families were no longer being torn apart, but aside from that, their lot was only marginally improved over that as slaves. And they resented having been enslaved by the whites they still had to live amongst.

Summary

Whites still bear the responsibility for what they did to the blacks they enslaved. Arguably, their subjugation and enslavement of the blacks was in some ways worse than what they did to Native American Indians, who were simply slaughtered or marginalized on reservations. In effect, they continued to treat not only the first generation of freed blacks but their future generations as second class citizens – a practice that continues to today for black Americans as a whole, despite some notable success stories, primarily in sports, politics, and entertainment and in the emergence of a small black middle class.

This singling out and mistreatment of an entire ethnic group has occurred because to the victors belong the spoils. And in the last 100 years, this benefit not only included the long-standing benefit of writing the history books, but the additional benefit of making iconic movies like *Birth of a Nation*. In this movie, good white robed Ku Klux Klansmen defended the nation from the scourge of evil blacks. The movie was acclaimed in the North as well as the South.

Thus, whites did free the slaves, at least legally, but, once freed, whites feared them. The aftermath of the Civil War might have been the appropriate time for reparations to blacks, but the country was broke, and whites felt they had done more than enough for blacks.

We can't change any of this history, but we can be more aware of what happened and try to understand how blacks and Southern whites came to the disparate attitudes they hold. Change for the better depends on that understanding, as does the desire to Make America Great Again.

Aspects of this racial divide, dating back to colonial times, continued after the Civil War to the present. The next chapter discusses what happened since black emancipation.

CHAPTER 2: THE RACIAL DIVIDE: OUR BLEAK PRESENT

It wasn't an easy life up North for blacks fleeing the Jim Crow South. When factories had to cut back or close, blacks suffered the most, since they were the first to lose work and quickly sink into poverty.

In most U.S. cities, they also faced rampant segregation, because each ethnic group was most comfortable in its own homogeneous neighborhood. While blacks were undoubtedly most comfortable around other blacks, the neighborhoods where they lived became the poorest and most crime-ridden – with much of the crime due to impoverished conditions. Another later contributor to this concentration of poverty and crime was that the whites who could move escaped to the suburbs, leaving the inner cities to the poor blacks.

 Then, a hundred years after the Civil War, President Lyndon Baines Johnson declared a War on Poverty, followed soon afterward by affirmative action programs. Both the War on Poverty and these programs were well intentioned, but they were also subject to the law of unintended consequences. The War on Poverty resulted in a welfare system which trapped many poor blacks in a subsistence existence without sufficient incentive to improve their lot. Similarly, affirmative action provided the benefit of establishing a significant black middle class, but these blacks moved out of the inner cities, further impoverishing the black brethren they left behind, resulting in black ghettos. Once out of the 'hood, the middle class blacks began to relate more to their own success and that of the whites around them than to the blacks left behind in the 'hood, as happened with O.J. Simpson before his 1994 arrest.

The unintended consequence was that the increasingly impoverished 'hood became rife with crime, and more and more blacks were locked up, many for petty crimes, in the "Get Tough on Crime" pushes starting in the 1980s. An enormous number of blacks were imprisoned as a result, often with long sentences of many years for relatively minor offenses like a sharing some drugs with a friend. Their incarceration further decimated the 'hood and broke down families.

The prison statistics for black males are truly a national shame. As many as a third of all black men end up in prison at some point in their life. This high rate of imprisonment has given the United States the dubious distinction of imprisoning more people than any other country in the world, based either on total numbers or on the percent of the population in prison or jail.

Further exacerbating the problem of black males ending up without jobs or in prison is that more than two-thirds of all blacks born are raised by single moms.[3] Since so many black males are unemployed, involved in crime, or imprisoned, young black males raised by single moms have no good male role models to guide them to living a more productive life. As a result, they drop out of school, face extremely high unemployment rates, participate in a lot of violent crime, and feel harassed by cops, who believe they are appropriately responding to the high rate of crime in black neighborhoods.

No wonder blacks distrust cops, and no wonder cops distrust blacks. They co-exist in a very unstable relationship which can deteriorate rapidly in response to any incident, and frequently does. Whites, who have largely abandoned downtown areas of many cities in their flight to the suburbs, would just as soon not know what goes on in the 'hood, as long as it doesn't affect them.

This mix of black-police confrontation and middle class white apathy is toxic. It is as if the middle class whites inserted the police between themselves and the blacks, creating a powder keg that can blow up at any time.

Some Suggested Solutions

Is there any solution? No one solution will suffice, but several combined together might.

- Establish more community policing. More black cops need to be recruited to help police the high crime neighborhoods where they live. All police also need to be given special training in community interaction.

- Train police to take less forceful steps to calm down a suspect in order to make an orderly arrest.

- Screen police for personality characteristics they might have in common with cops who have killed innocent blacks or who have shot too quickly at suspects resisting arrest. Those personality types who are too quick to respond aggressively could be assigned to desk duties or low crime neighborhoods. This will further reduce racial incidents between police and blacks.

- Encourage the formation of neighborhood watches in the black community, at least during daytime hours.

- Provide convicts with skills and training in prison to survive the harsh reality of re-entry into society. Otherwise, as measured by high recidivism rates, they are likely to wind up back in prison instead of becoming productive members of society. Many good programs exist to help them learn skills for success, and the prison staff need to know about them, so they can help guide prisoners into these opportunities to build skills and achieve success in legitimate jobs after they leave prison.

- Follow up pre-release programs with post-prison release support programs and support groups to help ex-cons find jobs and adjust to life outside prison.

- Encourage community members to think of additional approaches that might help to reintegrate convicts back into society, as well as guide black youths to leave behind a life of crime and adopt a more productive life.

- Provide young blacks raised by single moms better male role models than unsavory boyfriends, pimps, drug dealers, and gang members. In *The Price of Justice in America*, I suggested Barack Obama and Colin Powell could serve such roles, to which I would add sportsmen like Kareem Abdul-Jabbar, Michael

Jordan and Shaquille O'Neal. These well-known personalities could also be supplemented by the personal touch of some Big Brothers who extricated themselves from the ghettos.

- Provide young black girls better access to long-term contraceptives that would decrease the extremely high rate of teen pregnancies which trap single moms in the welfare system. Michelle Obama could inspire them to demand more of themselves, as could Oprah and Venus and Serena Williams.

- Establish federal, state and local tax incentives to start businesses providing more jobs in urban ghettos. This could include supermarkets in so-called food deserts and be coupled to greater police presence.

CHAPTER 3: THE RACIAL DIVIDE: DESEGREGATION AND AFFIRMATIVE ACTION

Although tackling violent crime in high crime urban communities suggests that this problem is predominantly a black problem, discrimination against blacks by whites has been a constant source of friction.

What is the source of that friction currently? Slavery has been ended for well over a century, and so has the Civil War. Certainly some whites are bigots, but they are in the minority.

The main reason for the friction is likely due to the lingering effects of desegregation. Cultural and economic differences between different groups likely added to the natural tendency of different groups to self-segregate. Desegregation flew in the face of that tendency and resulted in major friction, and the lingering effects of desegregation have persisted.

Desegregation was intended to provide a means toward a long-term greater integration of the races. It was based on the presumption that children of different races growing up together would not be subject to the same sort of racial intolerance as their parents.

Yet desegregation in the 50s, 60s and 70s caused a white backlash. Whites displayed some of their most intense feelings of hatred in response to the bussing of black students in places like Little Rock, Chicago, and Boston, among many other cities. In hindsight, this reaction could have been predicted. White parents particularly resented and resisted having their children bussed out of their neighborhoods with decent schools to faraway poor schools with large minorities. Even when desegregation was carried out, students from different races still tended to self-segregate, though at least they became more familiar with and perhaps less fearful of each other, rather than remaining ignorant.

The Difficulty of Ending Segregation

Segregation may be difficult to ever stop. Most U.S. cities are carved into ethnic neighborhoods, because people from different ethnic backgrounds prefer to preserve their culture and easy access to ethnic foodstuffs. Even blacks often prefer to remain among their own. It would take massive governmental intervention of the kind mandated in Singapore, where nearly everyone lives in nice public housing and is subject to governmental regulation, to produce the kind of positive change promised by desegregation. That certainly is unlikely to happen here.

Yet for those willing to move in among people of a different race or ethnicity, the barriers should be lowered. Unfortunately, whites are too often ignorant of the plight of blacks and sometimes too smug in thinking themselves superior. Our reputation as a cultural melting pot is due to a great extent to our ability to embrace hard-working immigrants who want to improve their children's chances to lead a good life. By the same token, whites should consider hard working blacks who can afford to move into middle class white communities in the same light as hard-working immigrants, rather than just judging them by their skin color. For the same reason, whites should not abandon neighborhoods after a few blacks or immigrants move in. If they stayed, housing prices would be less likely to depreciate.

While racial tension has never stopped simmering, the current backlash of angry whites appears to be largely economic in origin. Middle class wages have remained frozen for many years, and job insecurity is the new norm. Liberals sympathize with the plight of minorities and promote diversity at the same time that they heap scorn on struggling conservative whites who also face economic hardship. Whites waiting for a chance to improve their lot have sometimes found their way blocked by quotas established due to affirmative action. This has caused major resentment, and the election of Barack Obama, a recipient of affirmative action himself, exacerbated feelings of hostility of whites against blacks.

Possible Modifications of Affirmative Action

Times of economic hardship have always tended to most seriously affect minorities. Consequently, a moratorium on affirmative action in hiring during an economic downturn would be devastating for blacks economically and thus counterproductive.

A reduction of affirmative action in higher education might seriously slow any progress toward reducing the social and financial inequality between the races. However, higher education acceptance of black students through affirmative action could also require some form of community service in poor black communities as payback, especially for financial scholarships or loans.

Likewise, new black police hired by affirmative action might be required to serve and live in high crime communities. There is little doubt that neighborhood policing, especially when police officers live where they serve, reduces conflict and friction between cops and blacks.

What about minorities left behind in the urban ghettos? How could they be compensated?

Perhaps cities, states and the federal government could establish a joint sponsorship of programs proven to benefit slum dwellers in the inner cities, with the amount of support determined by the numbers of minorities locally hired by employers. Such an approach has already been instituted successfully in some locales. More housing vouchers and greater housing assistance for those in extreme poverty would certainly help.

What about whites suffering from perceived reverse discrimination?

Employers could be required to document all of their affirmative action hiring decisions in return for protecting or exempting them from reverse discrimination lawsuits instituted when employers favor a black applicant over a white one. Then whites who can demonstrate the loss of a job opportunity due to affirmative action could be compensated by qualifying for increased or longer term unemployment benefits. They could also be given preferential consideration for employment by being given affirmative action eligibility themselves.

Learning from the Military

Another idea to promote integration might be to use as a model the military's success in molding racially desegregated teams that function well in performing their mission. These teams are organized based on creating a team with the needed skills, since the military does not employ affirmative action. Accordingly, its experience provides a great testament to the benefits of racial integration, since this blending of different ethnic and racial groups shows how mixed groups not only can get along but can learn and grow from an introduction to each other's cultures and ideas.

To a great extent the military's emphasis on teamwork contributed to acceptance of minority groups in the unit. By the same token, it is likely that a greater emphasis on teamwork in job performance would similarly be beneficial for integrating the workforce.

Still another possibility for furthering integration might be providing more pre-job training for unskilled workers or for prisoners about to be released. Such a program might likewise be modeled after the military's approach, which is based on desegregation in a boot camp-type training. Rather than employing affirmative action to gain preconceived results, each recruit would be considered equally and would be judged based on performance alone, with no special dispensation due to being in a particular racial or ethnic group. Moreover, it is likely that private sources would contribute to supporting such training efforts because individuals would be judged on merit and skills in order to prepare them for jobs in different industries.

CHAPTER 4: THE NATIONALITY AND LANGUAGE DIVIDE

Our porous Southern border has resulted in a prolonged influx of illegal immigrants over the years such that it is now estimated that there are over 11 million illegal Hispanic immigrants in the U.S. Many were desperately seeking sanctuary from horrific violence in Mexico and Central America, and many more were simply seeking a better life for themselves and their families in the face of very high unemployment in their countries of origin. Many Hispanics also came to work here just to send money back to their families. Often they take jobs that Anglos would disdain – backbreaking farm labor at very low wages, while sleeping in subpar housing, or they work in the restaurant and housekeeping industries, again at very low wages. More problematic are day laborers in the construction industry, because these workers more directly compete with Americans for these jobs and are willing to work for less pay.

As a consequence, resentment among white Americans has grown, and on several fronts. As mentioned, although most of the jobs they take do not deprive Americans of employment and do support the economy, Hispanic immigrants do take away some desirable jobs, such as in the homebuilding and construction industry, and reduce the wages paid at others. Another gripe is that illegal immigrants take big bites out of our social services, as in healthcare and in education. They avoid medical care because they cannot afford it. Because they wait until they are seriously ill, they arrive at Emergency Departments requiring very expensive treatments. Because they have more children than Anglos, their children are consuming an ever increasing share of the national education budget. Affirmative action has also included Hispanics, another source of Anglo resentment.

But probably the biggest gripe of all is that Hispanics speak a different language and often make little attempt to assimilate. Like most immigrants from other cultures, they are more comfortable among their own, as witnessed by the myriad of ethnic neighborhoods in our major cities. First generation immigrants experience some difficulties adjusting to the new culture in the U.S., but for the most part they manage. Their children, second generation immigrants, have an easier time, since they are educated in U.S. schools and are often indistinguishable from U.S. citizens in terms of their English ability and even accents.

However, Hispanics have been treated differently. Bilingual education has been permitted and even encouraged in certain communities. While this may expedite initial education of immigrant children, it results in a diversion of education funds away from the children of Anglo citizens. And bilingual education may have slowed the progress of these children in assimilating into our culture. This is a pity, since Hispanic family values conform far better to those of American conservatives than to those of American liberals.

Anglo resentment of Hispanics has made immigration reform much more difficult, despite the agreed-upon need for so-called comprehensive immigration reform. No one agrees what constitutes comprehensive, except that it has to include the 11 million immigrants who are undocumented. Many Anglos despise the notion that illegal immigrants be granted amnesty and prefer that they be deported or self-deport.

The Wall

Another point of contention is the border between the U.S. and Mexico, which has been a route for illegal immigration that has included drug traffickers and other criminals. The proposed building of a wall between the two countries has created even more tension. This has increased since President Trump has continued to support his campaign promise to build a very high wall along our entire Southern border. This proposal in turn has provoked resentment among Hispanics, both in the U.S. and in Mexico.

The Wall conjures up images of the Great Wall of China, which did not manage to keep out all foreign invaders, and now is just a tourist attraction.

In more recent times, walls have become both a physical barrier and an emotional issue. One only has to look at other walls elsewhere to see that.

The Wall dividing East and West Germany kept a defeated rogue nation divided for about 45 years and became a big emotional symbol dividing Capitalism and Communism, both for Germans and for the rest of the world. Unlike other walls, it was designed to keep its citizens in, not to keep outsiders out. It served its purpose but was hated. It has been laced with graffiti and has become another tourist attraction.

An even more recent example is the Wall dividing Israel and the West Bank. That wall, when coupled with perceived Israeli land grabs and no progress toward an independent Palestinian state, has caused extreme resentment among Palestinians. That resentment has, in turn, caused consequent condemnation in most of the international community.

So walls can work, but they come at a cost, both in public relations and financially. Furthermore, unless adequately manned or monitored, walls can be traversed by those healthy enough with ladders or ropes. Those in charge of securing the border actually advocate structures that permit visibility through them for better monitoring, which would probably reduce cost. But then consider that Mexicans have become expert at building tunnels to go underneath the border. Even Israelis have difficulty locating all the tunnels Palestinians have built along their short border. It will be much harder to locate all the tunnels that might be built along our 1800 mile border with Mexico.

However, none of this consideration about building a wall on the border takes into account that the flow of immigrants across the Southern border has diminished greatly in the last several years.[4] Border patrol apprehensions have diminished from over 1.6 million in 2000 to just over 130,000 in 2017, because the Mexican economy has flourished, reducing the total 6.9 million illegal Mexican immigrants down to 5.4 million as they return to Mexico.[5] Even so, there are more asylum seekers from Central America, including recent caravans, resulting in an increase in asylum-seeking families, which has overwhelmed our capability to manage them in aged facilities designed only for young male immigrants. Yet, in spite of all their efforts to staunch the immigration flow, Border Patrol still apprehended around a half million illegal immigrants in 2018.[6]

This large number of apprehensions increases the chances that a smaller number of dangerous criminals will evade detection and enter the country illegally. If the numbers of asylum seekers entering illegally were decreased by a wall or other border security, dangerous criminals would be provided less cover, and freed-up Border Patrol agents would be more likely to apprehend them.

Will Democrats give the President the billions of dollars that he wants to construct a wall? We know Mexico will never agree to pay for the cost of it. The Wall has also incensed Mexico and the vast majority of Hispanics, who make up 16% of the U.S. population. Given that this percentage represents about 50 million people, the majority of whom are legal immigrants, there may be a high political price to pay. The future price for Republicans may be even higher, when in a few decades whites become a minority in the U.S.

Fortunately, a new Mexican administration might be willing to work with the President and may house many of these asylum seekers until the courts rule on their asylum applications. With any luck, many of these immigrants will stay in Mexico, where they may be better absorbed into the Spanish-speaking Mexican culture. We should encourage their stay there as much as we can, even to the point of subsidizing any Mexican initiatives to accept these immigrants.

Alternatives to the Wall

There are alternatives to the Wall. Border Patrol agents recommend some sort of fencing and better monitoring. The President himself has proposed additional border patrol agents and slab metal fencing, which may make more sense than a tall concrete wall along the entire border.

Another possibility is that all this discussion of the wall and deportation will simply ratchet up fear in the Hispanic community -- fear of Immigration and Customs Enforcement (ICE) agents knocking on their doors in the middle of the night and fear of mass deportations. We will never be able to identify and deport all 11 million illegal immigrants, but we may be capable of generating enough fear in the Hispanic community that many will self-deport and return to a Mexico that is now better off than when they left it. The political price for such a strategy will be high, but probably no higher than building the Wall.

It might be an idea to revisit Bush-era proposals, even including possible difficult paths to citizenship, on devising some compromise for comprehensive immigration reform. Even with a current impasse between the President and Democrats on the wall, everyone agrees that the present immigration system is a mess in drastic need of overhaul. Unfortunately, the immigration dilemma will keep rearing its ugly head, if we don't come to some more comprehensive solution soon. What about a pathway to legal, non-voting status rather than citizenship for current illegal immigrants, perhaps coupled to some fines and an end of affirmative action for Hispanics?

CHAPTER 5: GEOGRAPHICAL AND POLITICAL DIVIDES

The numerous geographical and political divides in America represent another source of tension. These include divisions between North and South, the Coasts and Middle America, and rural and urban residents. In addition there are ethnic and generational divisions and divisions due to income inequality.

The North-South Divide

Even 150 years after the Civil War, the South is resentful. Whites in the South were humiliated. Their way of life was taken away from them. They had to endure free blacks. Northern carpetbaggers further ravaged the South economically.
But Southerners slowly got their revenge. After President Lyndon Baines Johnson, they virtually exiled Democrats from the South, yet more Southern Democrats became Presidents than Northern Democrats. The South has contributed mightily to the economic decline of the Rust Belt by recruiting companies with cheaper non-union labor. Southerners also form the Bible Belt and are considerably more conservative than most Northerners. While the South can reliably be counted on to vote Republican, the South doesn't make up enough of the country to elect a President by itself.

The Divide between the Coasts and Middle America

A second, more critical geographical distinction currently is that between the Midwest and the Coasts. It is reflected in the division between the red states (shown in white below), which largely vote conservative and Republican, and the blue states (shown in dark gray below), which largely vote liberal and Democratic, as indicated in the map of the 2016 Presidential election below.

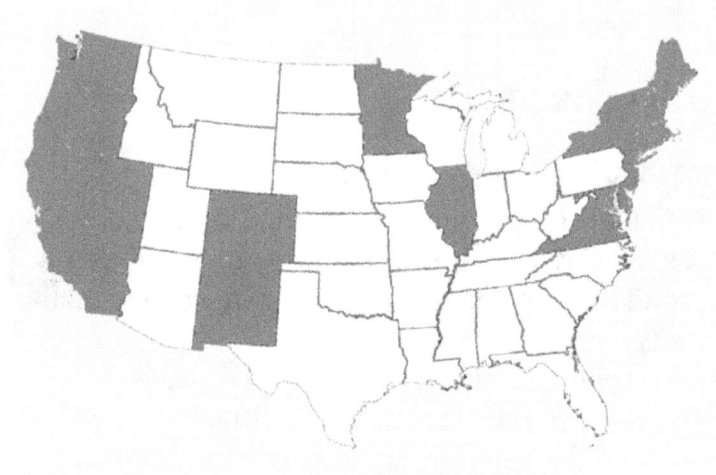

Pollsters have repeatedly shown similar results for the last few decades. Generally speaking, the Midwest and South reliably vote Republican, while the only states that reliably vote Democratic are those on the West Coast and East Coast in the Northeast. About the only reliably Democratic states in the Midwest are Minnesota and Illinois. Recently, most of the Rust Belt states voted for Donald Trump, and because of the power of the Electoral College, Trump won the Presidency by winning three key battleground states –

Wisconsin, Michigan, and Pennsylvania – by a slim 80,000 vote margin.

The Rural-Urban Divide

A third geographical divide is between rural and urban America. On electoral maps, this divide shows up in many states as a sea of red Republican-voting regions dotted with a few small blue Democratic-voting islands, as depicted in the map of counties below, where red counties are shown in light gray and blue counties in black.

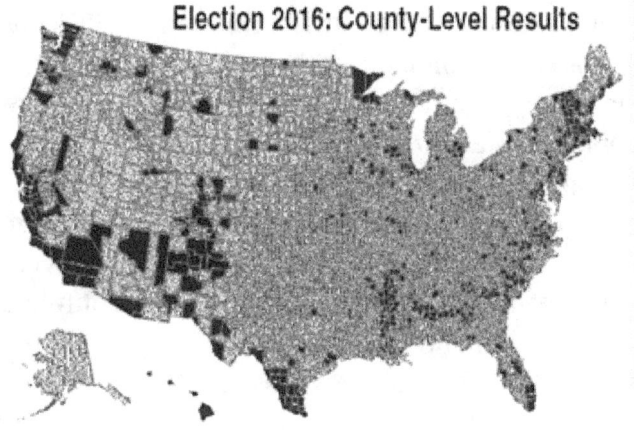

Election 2016: County-Level Results

This rural-urban divide is also played out in economic disparities between the two areas. Cities have traditionally represented the apex of our civilizations, as exemplified by Athens and Rome. This tradition has continued in Europe, which has maintained the vibrancy of its cities and made it difficult for immigrants to live there, but easier for them to live in impoverished suburbs.

In the U.S., the economic division between urban and rural areas is reversed, since many cities were abandoned by the white flight to the suburbs. U.S. cities remain business hubs, but their downtown areas are often deserted at nights and on weekends. This has been changing in some city neighborhoods where gentrification has been occurring, such as in "progressive" Boston, Seattle, New York, and San Francisco, where a downtown nightlife has flourished.

However, this increased infusion of wealth into certain areas has led to a division within these cities, since gentrification also excludes the poor. As a result, at the same time that parts of the cities have become a magnet for wealthy and well-paid high tech employees, the impoverished inner city slums have been growing in other parts of the same cities, due to the fallout from the growing divide between rich and poor in America. So gentrification may help reclaim downtown areas of some cities, but it does not result in significant desegregation. In fact, it can make things worse, much worse, such as in San Francisco, Oakland and some other metropolitan areas that are suffering from a crisis of insufficient housing, exploding housing costs, and a growing homeless problem marked by tent cities, drugs, and crime.

Rural America and urban America are completely different culturally, and this may be the most fundamental divide of all. Their values are vastly different. Rural America is more religious and more conservative. Rural Americans work longer hours, believe in self-sufficiency, and disdain handouts.

Rural America is much closer to nature and to the land, including farmlands and pasture. Rural America provides much of the food for urban America, which also receives imports from foreign countries.

By comparison, urban America provides most business, jobs, and shopping malls.

It costs much more to live in urban America, due to rapidly escalating real estate prices. Urban Americans get almost all of their food from the local supermarket or fast food franchises, whereas rural Americans can feed themselves less expensively by farming and hunting to supplement any store-bought food.

These divisions are much more than economic. They are based in deep social and cultural differences, too, since urban America tends to dismiss and disparage rural America for not keeping up with the times and having old-fashioned values. Conversely, rural America sees in urban America a world of chaos and corruption exemplified by the false values of Hollywood and materialism.

Some Suggested Solutions

Given this rural-urban divide, it may be more important to permit separate urban and rural rights than to emphasize the power of states' rights. The crime problem is very different in rural and urban America, largely because of the concentration of crime in urban America in the inner city slums. And given these differences, what may reduce crime in rural areas is much less likely to work in urban areas. Separate court systems may be appropriate for rural and urban America.

Recently, a group of city mayors has argued that they can make independent decisions about issues like immigration, crime, and even climate change, and then they can do what is best for their city rather than simply following federal guidelines. The first test of their proposed approach might be whether the Trump administration cuts off federal support for so-called "sanctuary cities," which have established policies to shield their mostly Hispanic immigrants from federal action designed to deport those immigrants to their country of origin.

Note, however, the following delicious irony. In 2016, rural Republicans chose as their candidate for the Presidency the very epitome of the successful urban real estate developer, someone whose basic values were unlikely to match their own. Then, in the 2016 election, it was this sea of rural Republicans which voted for this urban non-politician, whereas all the liberal Democratic urban islands voted against Donald J. Trump. The U.S. may not be as monolithic after all. The President has shown the way, at least in this instance.

The hyper-partisanship could also be reduced through some changes in the primary system, which the two political parties use to elect their Presidential candidates. Through these primaries, the members of each party vote to select the candidate for the general election. Unfortunately, these primaries have recently resulted in the selection of increasingly extreme candidates who fight to outdo one another in appealing to their party's base. That extremism could be reduced if independents were allowed to vote in the Presidential primaries instead of just registered party voters, which is currently allowed in many states.[7] If independents were allowed to vote for either party's candidates in all states, more moderate Presidential candidates willing to work with the other side would be increasingly likely to be selected.

CHAPTER 6: OTHER DIVIDES

Ethnic Divides

Naturally, there are other divides as well. To some extent, different ethnicities colonized different parts of the country. This may explain why my wife of German extraction assimilated well in Texas, which had a lot of German immigrants in the 1800s, but she has only barely been accepted in Arkansas, which has a lot of Scots-Irish.

For more on this issue of ethnic divides, consult Colin Woodard's book *American Nations*[8] and related articles, which emphasize the different cultural attitudes toward guns and violence. These cultural attitudes arise from ethnic differences and have contributed to the higher rates of assault deaths in the Deep South than in New England.

Generational Divides

My book *American Justice?* recounts the horrible treatment my wife encountered here in Arkansas, but while different ethnicities between my wife and our neighbors may have played a role, a generational divide was most likely more significant. Members of our generation who were raised by European parents experienced much stricter discipline in growing up and were required to be more respectful of their elders, whereas parents in later generations have become far more lenient toward their children.

Aside from the difficulties we encountered from the criminal justice system and from younger neighbors due to their lack of respect for elders, age discrimination was a likely factor, too, in that our society celebrates youth and often shows little respect for those who are older, other than those in high positions of authority.

Age discrimination affects a lot of people. It's been called a moral embarrassment because most workers over 50 have been fired or forced out of their jobs at one point or another, and our politicians have done nothing about it.[9] It's certainly true that businesses prefer to hire younger staff to whom they can pay lower salaries. Moreover, older Americans are generally unable to work as fast or be as productive as younger workers, yet often they are paid much more due to their seniority. They also add more expenses for society, since they qualify for Medicare and Social Security which younger workers don't.

Another source of tension is that the individual mandate of Obamacare was instituted in order to have healthy younger Americans help pay for the greater medical care required for older Americans. Then, too, many of the elderly live in comfortable retirement communities and don't wish to have any of these benefits pared, even when future generations will not be able to support those programs or enjoy those same benefits themselves. No wonder there is tension between the generations.

Each subsequent generation has been pigeonholed and labeled: baby boomers, gen-Xers, millennials, and centennials. The particular labels don't matter, but the labeling process reflects the great divide between the generations that is especially marked in much of the U.S.

How to Understand the Generational Divide

Currently, only two groups appear to really understand the different motivations, aspirations, and fears that drive each of these generational categories.

One group consists of businessmen and advertisers who are marketing products and their advertisements to specific groups, because they need this understanding to position and market their products successfully.

The other group consists of pollsters who gather data for the benefit of politicians, since the politicians need to target their message to appeal to these different groups.

Thus, the only way the rest of us will recognize and come to understand our generational differences is if we call on advertisers and pollsters to educate us.

How did we develop this generational divide and what can we do about it? One way is to recognize the forces drawing us apart and take some steps to overcome them.

One factor is the emphasis on individualism in the United States and another is the high level of mobility, which tends to break up the family. For example, U.S. businesses encourage and reward mobility on the part of their workers. Consequently, the U.S. family is by and large a nuclear one: only two generations in the household -- the parents and children.

By contrast, Hispanic, European and Asian families here and in their home countries are far more likely to have several generations living under the same roof or within close proximity to each other. That closeness leads to greater understanding, appreciation, respect, and cooperation among the generations that is sorely lacking for U.S. families.

Today's parents raise their children more permissively than the way they were raised with greater discipline. One recent article indicated that today's parents don't even want their children to be around their grandparents too much, because of these differences in opinions about child rearing.[10] That sort of generational divide is very sad and destructive.

Family-owned businesses are also affected. For example, the era of the family farm is largely over. The absence of other work nearby has led to younger generations of farm families abandoning the land in favor of greater job opportunities in cities, rendering the family farm an endangered species. Putting further pressure on the family farm is economic pressure from large corporate farm operations which are able to generate greater efficiencies of scale than a small farm, thereby rendering the family farm a nearly extinct species.

Intergenerational living under the same roof doesn't happen very much here, despite a trend for millennials who have trouble finding jobs to return to the family roost temporarily. As a result, individuals of one generation tend to associate with others of the same generation and to become increasingly isolated and less understanding of the needs and wishes of other generations.

How to Overcome the Generational Divide

To overcome these divides, grown children of retired parents should be encouraged, perhaps with tax credits, to take in their parents, if their parents are willing to live with them. Grandparents are a great resource to help in raising children. Retirees are often suffering financially for lack of sufficient retirement savings, but their children could step in and pay them back a measure for their upbringing by taking care of their parents in those parents' declining years. Conversely, parents in their empty nest years, generally in their late 30s, 40s, and 50s, might help their children who are struggling financially by taking them in while they get on their feet.

Much greater attention should also be given to the ways that Hispanic families benefit from several generations living under the same roof. Even if it is not feasible for most Anglos to accommodate their parents, they may learn some of the positive benefits of greater association with those of other generations. The recognition of these benefits could be accomplished by encouraging volunteer work dedicated specifically to helping those of other generations.

Another way to help heal the split is that generational diversity in neighborhoods should be encouraged by more active neighborhood associations, both in face-to-face meetings as well as on line. These associations could identify needs and recognize the contributions of individuals of one generation in assisting individuals of another generation.

Income Inequality

Another major source of division is the growing income inequality in America. Just recently a charity soliciting donations pointed out that eight super wealthy individuals own as much wealth as the poorest half of the people in the world! That poorest half is composed of 3.6 billion members, while 6 of the 8 richest are Americans: Jeff Bezos, Bill Gates, Warren Buffett, Mark Zuckerberg, Larry Ellison and Michael Bloomberg. This is certainly a stark picture of the vast gulf between rich and poor caused by the great inequality divide.

Listening to the President, you'd think the U.S. has lost its greatness. In certain respects, it has not. A Global

Wealth Report 2015 by Allianz, a major financial services firm, lists the top 10 countries in terms of their percentages of total global wealth:

United States	- 41.6%	France	- 3.5%
China	- 10.5%	Canada	- 3.0%
Japan	- 8.9%	Italy	- 2.9%
U.K.	- 5.6%	Australia	- 2.0%
Germany	- 3.9%	South Korea	- 1.9%

    As you can see, the U.S. holds almost half the world's wealth. No other country even comes close, not even China. The sum of the top 4 countries in Western Europe (15.9%) doesn't even generate half of our wealth. No wonder 6 of the world's 8 richest people are Americans. This might be a list we Americans could be proud of.

    But the same report indicates that the U.S. is also at the top of the list in terms of income inequality. This is not a recent phenomenon.

    The Center of Budget and Policy Priorities has estimated that since 1979, households at the top 1% of income have had their incomes appreciate by 242%, compared to only 78% for the next 19% of top income earning households, 79% for the bottom 20%, and just 46% for the middle 60% (the real middle class). This has resulted in the following pie chart distribution of incomes by 2016, and the one below which shows an even more unequal distribution of wealth[11]:

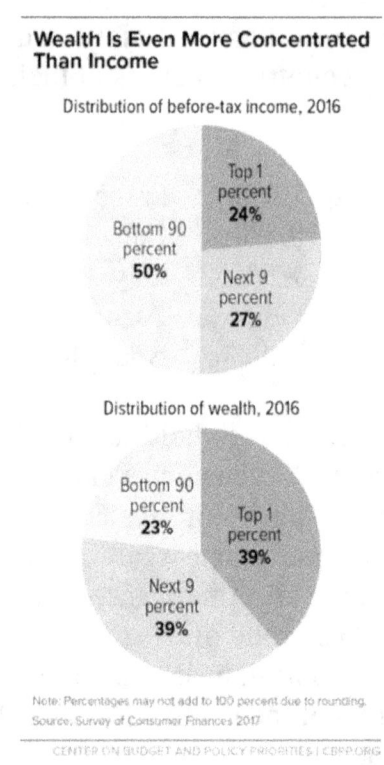

Why Is There So Much Inequality in America?

American society has a lot of income inequality. In part, this economic divide is due to our pride in our system of capitalism and our values of individualism and freedom. Our ideal is that individuals can make themselves who they want to be by having clear goals for success and hard work, and they can ignore the real barriers many face to getting ahead. These barriers include not having the funds to secure an education necessary to move up the economic ladder. Our ideal also downplays the real advantages that come from having a high income family which is well connected.

At the same time, we disparage others who are not successful by claiming they have certain flaws that prevent them from getting ahead and so deserve whatever bad experience comes their way. For example, we pride ourselves on the fruit of our labor and don't feel that those lazier than ourselves deserve as much.

Meanwhile, many accept the proposition that the wealthy can use their money to control job opportunities for the poor and believe that trickle-down economics will actually lead to more jobs for workers, rather than further enriching those who are already wealthy. On the other hand, those who are disadvantaged don't believe that they are fairly reaping economic rewards, so management and labor are frequently at odds with each other.

Witness the ongoing debate about raising the minimum wage. Business owners are largely opposed, while workers are pushing for a higher living wage, especially in cities that have become increasingly expensive for workers to live there, such as rapidly gentrifying San Francisco.

We thrive on the capitalist system and don't want to become as socialist as Western Europe with its expensive social safety net or as Bernie Sanders and Elizabeth Warren would like. However, we tend to overlook those who lose out as a result of this system in which the rich keep getting richer and the poor poorer. At the same time, the middle class is whittled away and many formerly middle class individuals and families become impoverished. If this trend continues, our capitalist system could be jeopardized. Tucker Carlson has argued that great divides between rich and poor resulted in the ascendancy of Hugo Chavez, a socialist dictator, in Venezuela, the kind of situation we can't allow to happen here. He also argued that the election of President Trump may presage the advent of a similar situation in the U.S.[12]

So shouldn't we be asking when is enough money enough? Is there a point at which government or wealthy individuals themselves should intervene in order to help redistribute some of the wealth from those on the top, so those on the bottom can better survive and work towards their own success?

There is no doubt that great entrepreneurs have improved our lives and capabilities, and they should be rewarded. Steve Jobs did not live an opulent lifestyle, and neither does Warren Buffett. Wouldn't a billion dollars be enough? In fact, many billionaires seem to have come to this conclusion and are seeking to give their money away to worthwhile causes. One prominent example is Bill Gates, who has stopped trying to make money and is trying to figure out how best to give it away through the Bill and Melinda Gates Foundation. That's a lot of work, so Warren Buffett, asked Gates to give his money away as well. Almost certainly some of Gates' donations have been less successful than others, but then that is the nature of creating a system to offer money to needy individuals or causes.

There has also been a move by Warren Buffett to have wealthy philanthropists pledge to give away at least 50% of their fortunes. That may be admirable, but did these wealthy Americans need to amass so much wealth that they didn't know what to do with it? Is there something about our system that is so imbalanced that too much money goes to those who are already very wealthy or that some corporate leaders make 300 time as much as their employees?

These fabulously successful entrepreneurs reach a point where they realize they need to do something philanthropic with the money they generated, to put the excess money they don't need to some good use. They have much less experience and proficiency in that area. I say this despite the fact that I support Mark Zuckerberg and Priscilla Chen's pledge to commit $3 billion to cure disease. Their effort has started by rewarding high risk, high reward research that the National Institutes of Health (NIH) is unlikely to fund.

On the other hand, Facebook has been criticized for its dissemination of private information to businesses, foreign governments, and even the Trump campaign. And Microsoft and Apple have been criticized for their outsourcing to China for cheap labor.[13] All three and other Silicon Valley enterprises have been accused of monopolistic practices.

One question many ask is why super rich individuals feel a need to keep on making more and more money and never seem satisfied with enough. They may be good at it, but is that any reason to continue *ad infinitum*? Certainly they may need to reinvest in a successful business enterprise to keep it going, so I'm not suggesting that individuals and businesses shouldn't benefit from having healthy profit margins. Rather, I'm talking about a psychological addiction to making money that may be akin to an addiction to gambling. Gambling addictions are destructive to the individual with the addiction. An addiction to making money[14] would fall in the same category, known as process addictions.[15] It may be less destructive to the individual but could be quite destructive to society.

Some Ways to Fix the Income Inequality Problem

I suggest two possible remedies for income inequality.

First, re-education, training centers, and retreats should be established for those few individuals who are completely consumed with making money for its own sake. While these are designed to be treatment centers, they should be given another more socially acceptable name for those in power, so they don't have to think of themselves as having any kind of disturbance requiring psychological treatment.

Since these centers would only be designed for an extremely small group of people – the super-wealthy who are guided by making money to the exclusion of other motivators, we probably wouldn't need more than one or two high-quality retraining centers.

Funding for such a center should be very high, since its occupants are used to luxury, and probably the funding could come from the very rich, since they have the means to pay for the very best. As in other education, training, and treatment centers, like-minded individuals with a similar compulsion, could empathize with each other and help each other along the journey toward changing their way of life, much like groups like Gamblers Anonymous help individuals maintain their commitment to change and self-improvement.

How would we encourage these individuals to go to such a center? One way might be to promote the opportunity to network with each other and exchange ideas on how to make money as well as to give it away. Another approach would be to convince gambling addicts that they need help to break their obsessive money-making habit.

Second, government could finally overhaul and simplify the tax system, something conservatives have long advocated. This change in the tax law should leave the millionaires alone to continue making money and creating jobs. However, it should establish some sort of cap to limit individuals from amassing wealth beyond a certain sum, whether that is $1 billion, $5 billion or $10 billion. Any additional income earned would have 92% of it turned over to the government for social programs or to a choice among specific charities from a government-approved list. Why 92%? Because that was the top tax rate during the Eisenhower administration for those earning over what would be about $3.5 million now.[16] Remember, that was when America was truly great--shortly after World War II. And since there is an even greater problem with wealth inequality, legislators should consider capping the amount of extraordinary wealth that can be parked overseas or passed on to heirs.

The social programs to be considered should be ones for the poor that have been demonstrated to be effective in raising them out of poverty through their own work and initiative, thereby further reducing income inequality. What should the criteria be for what charities are eligible for such donations? These donations should either benefit everyone, or those in greatest need, since this would decrease income inequality the most. If so desired, the government-approved list could require that all such charities put America first.

These suggestions have focused on those at the upper end of the income scale. What about those at the lower end? In Chapter 3 in relation to slum housing, I mentioned housing vouchers and other forms of housing assistance.

The more than half a million homeless are a serious problem in the U.S.[17] Most have no income at all. Those who work cannot afford housing. Many must be treated for mental illness and institutionalized or given housing. The rest are also in acute need of housing. Tourists coming from abroad who encounter the homeless are unlikely to go back to their countries believing America is great.

However, the nearly million renters evicted annually represent an even greater problem. Eviction severely traumatizes their households and leaves them only one step away from homelessness.[18] They have to scramble to find even less suitable housing and spend more than half their income on that housing, which leaves them insufficient funds to afford food or utilities. Banks rarely lend for mortgages that would cost the homeowner more than 35% of their income. Aside from the over 4.5 million households receiving housing assistance currently, it has been estimated that between 7 million and 17.6 million other households with low income are in need of affordable housing.[19,20]

Increasing the number of housing vouchers could help. It has been estimated that this would cost $22.5 billion, but would provide stability that would greatly enhance the ability of the recipients to hold down their jobs.[21] Perhaps the taxes on the very richest billionaire Americans could be reserved for additional housing assistance for the poorest Americans.

Subsidizing renters is another approach that may work in certain locations where there is plenty of housing, but in many others a subsidy might not work if there is a housing shortage. In that case, landlords might not be willing to rent to renters with subsidies. Even if they do, rental prices might rise further because of the housing shortage. Therefore, a better solution might be to construct more housing. As Tyler Cohen, has written in "Disappointing Economics" in the *Bloomberg News,* "The best and most sustainable way of producing cheaper housing is to build more homes and apartments. The resulting increase in supply will cause prices to fall in many neighborhoods. There will be more housing, more choice of housing, and more people in homes and apartments. That is basic supply and demand, with supply doing the active work."[22]

A Threatening Gender Divide

There has always been a gender gap in pay, and there certainly was a gender gap in the 2016 election, since Hillary Clinton attracted many female supporters hoping the glass ceiling would be broken, as it had for African Americans by Obama. Allegations of sexual misconduct against Donald Trump abounded in the campaign.

In the past year, the divide between males and females became much stronger because of more sexual misconduct allegations. This may have been a result of the Me Too movement, but it certainly picked up steam beginning with allegations against movie producer Harvey Weinstein, costing him his position. Numerous politicians and celebrity dignitaries fell prey by following him, including Al Franken, Charley Rose and Matt Lauer. Bill Cosby was even thrown in prison. Women cheered and men began to feel they could all be victims of false accusations.

Worst of all were the allegations made against Justice Brett Kavanaugh. These were likely mainly politically motivated, and they tore apart the confirmation process, cast doubt on the ability of the Supreme Court to avoid partisanship, and further widened the divide between men and women. The gap was so wide that many families must have been affected even more than the current political divide, with divisions breaking apart husbands and wives, brothers and sisters, and parents and their children.

CHAPTER 7: WHY WE STILL NEED EACH OTHER

Whether they realize it or not, to one extent or another those on each side of these divides need each other. The need is not always mutual. Without a doubt, the poor need the rich more than the rich need the poor. The older generation certainly needs and should get help from the younger generations. Although the younger generations often manage on their own better than their parents do, some do need an occasional assist from mom and dad. By the same token, parents of younger children could benefit from having live-in or nearby grandparents to help raise children.

Different ethnic regions of the country and the North/South divide still have some need of each other. The South benefits from the North because it remains part of the much greater and more powerful United States of America, rather than having to fend for itself. The North still needs the South for some of its agricultural products and lower cost manufacturing. The Coasts need the Midwest for their farms and livestock, and the Midwest needs the Coasts in order to ship their products internationally and to import the products it needs. Heaven help the U.S. if the West Coast decided to secede.

The greatest co-dependence is exhibited by rural and urban America. Rural America would not survive without hungry urban America there to buy its goods. Urban America could only survive without rural America if it imported all its food, which would seriously raise urban food prices.

Yet these two Americas do not appreciate each other, and that leads to the disaffection exhibited by our two party political system. Urbanites need to appreciate the hard work and work ethic of rural Americans. Rural Americans need to acknowledge their dependence on Urban America for consumption of their bounty, for commerce in general, and for tax supports. And, as pointed out earlier, Rural Americans have to thank Urban America for providing them the President they elected.

The Increasing Uncivility and Toxicity of the System

This two party system recently has become increasingly uncivil and toxic. That toxicity has led to tribalism, whereby politicians in each party show allegiance to their tribe more than to their constituents or country. Cooperation is nearly nonexistent. Collaborators, a dirty word in World War II, have been eclipsed by competitors, a trademark of our capitalist society. Votes like this one on Obamacare certainly weren't bipartisan.

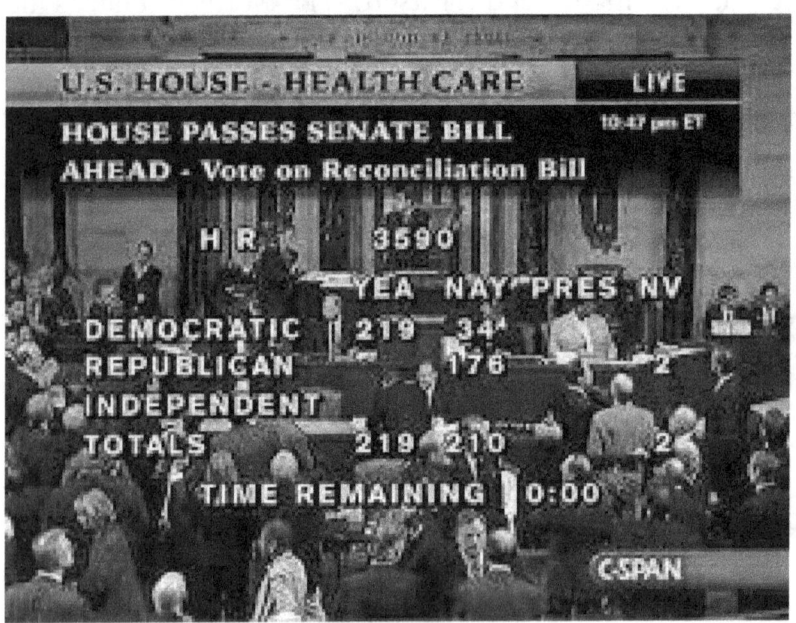

Thus, bipartisanship seems to be dead or dying, splitting us further apart, with the risk of a new Civil War, which some journalists even write about.[23] Another reason for this incivility and toxicity is that money has become paramount, and, as discussed in the previous chapter, no amount seems to be enough, even for the richest among us. That greed has created increasing economic inequality and much suffering, anguish, and anger. Compromise could be a solution,[24] but tribalism fights even that. The country is divided, yet each side, in turn, claims a "mandate" with every presidential election, even if they lose the popular vote. Most recently this has been reflected in the loss of Democrats like Al Gore and Hillary Clinton, due to the Electoral College system, despite winning the popular vote.

The Electoral College, whatever its merits, has unfortunately deprived most Americans of the value of their vote, whether they live in Red States or Blue States. In both cases, their votes are taken for granted. Only votes of citizens of so-called battleground states are seriously courted or contested, because only their votes can sway an election. In the 2016 election, the 10 consensus battleground states had a combined total of 132 electoral college votes out of a total of 538 (only 24.5%). The remaining 75% of voters were effectively disenfranchised; their issues didn't count as much. The Electoral College should be reformed so as to make Presidential candidates appeal to voters in all states.

The absence of a willingness to compromise is the single biggest roadblock to making America great again, as former Republican Senator Alan Simpson of Wyoming has warned:

> "America now finds itself the bound prisoner of congressional gridlock. We all honestly

know what we must do, but just cannot find the common purpose to do what is obviously necessary to pull the country on the road back to financial well-being and long term prosperity."[25]

Ultimately this could lead to the collapse of the political system, which probably cannot long endure favorability ratings under 20%. The election of President Trump demonstrated voter disaffection with both political parties. While over a million disaffected women came to Washington to protest the Trump presidency, it is likely that a million Trump supporters might have descended on Washington with their own march of disapproval had Hillary Clinton won.

Some Ways to Reform the System

Is there anything that can turn that divisiveness and intergroup hostility around? There is, but it will take extensive work beginning with seeking mutual understanding and compromise. Each side has to attempt to understand what most matters to and motivates the other side, whether older vs. younger, rich vs. poor, white vs. black, southern vs. northern, rural vs. urban, conservative vs. liberal, or Republican vs. Democrat. If we don't seek this understanding and compromise, the country will continue to swing back and forth between extremist positions on the two sides, and the hostilities might even escalate further, resulting in severe economic and social damage to our country.

What is really needed is a more objective look into the issues that divide the two sides to help decide how to break the impasses. In *The Price of Justice in America*, I started to consider these possible solutions. In that book, I used correlation analysis to come to the conclusion that liberals were mistaken about gun ownership being the primary cause of violent crime and homicides. I found instead that poor blacks in urban ghettos contributed the most to violent crime, and that blacks needed to concentrate more on how to reduce black-on-black killings, which considerably outnumber police killings of blacks, the focus of the Black Lives Matter movement.

If the current need to raise funds for reelection efforts could be reduced, that would help, since both sides are at fault in spending too much money on these races. But neither side in power is willing to change the status quo. They each seem to try to raise more and more money, believing that the campaign with the most money is more likely to win, and campaign debt can be paid off after the election. But a huge spending spree at election time doesn't always work. Witness the loss of Hillary Clinton, who lost despite spending much more than Donald Trump. And several millionaire businessmen like Mike Huffington and Meg Whitman spent millions on their failed bids for office in California.

As a result of these financial excesses, campaign finance reform is very badly needed. This can reduce the corroding influence of money from big money donors seeking favorable treatment and the wastefulness of huge sums spent on elections by both parties.

Aside from these considerations, campaign finance reform to reduce expenses would cut down on the time legislators spend at phone banks soliciting contributions. Instead, they would have considerably more time to attend to the people's business.[26] One can only hope for campaign finance reform, now that Donald Trump has shown that a candidate can win while being outspent by far more money raised by Hillary Clinton.

Changes in procedural rules might also be implemented to encourage bipartisan action and compromise, as suggested by some political insiders. Unfortunately, such changes can only be made by D.C. politicians, who don't seem inclined to make any changes to rein in political influence.

Still, there is an outcry for change that was manifested in the 2016 election, and it should be heeded by the two parties in order to gain popular support for what Congress and the President are doing. Otherwise, the next years will only be filled with more upheavals, especially in light of divisive concerns that the Presidential election may have been undermined and possibly delegitimized by Russian hacking. Still other sources of upheaval are the liberal outcries regarding Republican insistence on voter I.D. requirements and the repeal of Obamacare.

The outcry for change was not only exhibited by Trump supporters, but also by Bernie Sanders supporters before he lost the Democratic primary to Hillary Clinton. The public is angry about gridlock in Washington and the failure of federal politicians to serve Main Street instead of Wall Street. They don't agree with the huge salaries and bonuses for CEOs, when their own standard of living is stagnant or receding. They have shown that they are desperate enough to elect a very wealthy non-politician as President. There is also concern that President Trump's appointment of other billionaires to cabinet level positions may signal less willingness to help the little guy on Main Street than Candidate Trump's campaign promises.

Both political parties are in disarray as a result of the public anger and the 2016 election. Traditional Democrats, who came out on the short end of the stick when Hillary Clinton lost, will face a serious challenge from former Bernie Sanders supporters, perhaps with support from Elizabeth Warren. Dozens of Democrats are expected to declare their candidacy for the Presidency in the coming year.

The Republicans coalesced under President Trump's leadership following the 2016 election. Only a few weeks before the election, their party was very divided and could become so again if the Mueller probe, the Government Shutdown, or voter disaffection derails the President. The President and many Republicans have still been beset by continuing scandals about corruption and bad behavior. This is reflected in the continued charges and investigations of Russian hacking and most recently by the disgracefully rancorous Senate hearings on the confirmation of Justice Kavanaugh to the Supreme Court and a consequent backlash of women voters in the 2018 elections. Republicans lost control of the House in 2018.

Conservatives also face being drowned by a Tsunami, when whites become a minority in the country in a few decades. If conservatives don't reach out sincerely and successfully to blacks, Hispanics, and women, no amount of voter registration requirements or mass deportations will prevent the flood of anger that is likely to be unleashed at the voting booth in the future. Even before that, there could be mass protests, further escalations of resistance, and even violence on a recurring basis that could undermine the economy and lead to America's decline on the world stage. At least two countries, Russia and China, are positioning themselves to take on the mantle of world leadership.

All told, there are a lot of reasons for Americans of different political stripes to work together to achieve a more united country to contribute to the success of all. Even the conservative-leaning U.S. Chamber of Commerce has recently endorsed using measures of bipartisanship in their scoring of legislators. They hope to foster greater bipartisan solutions and a better functioning government in order to reduce legislative stalemates that are detrimental to business.[27]

Even the "fake" news media could play a role. They're not all fake, though they are all hyperpartisan. They pretend to show both sides of an issue by inviting spokespersons for the other side to participate in discussions or debates, but you always know whose side the TV station and its viewers are on. Rather than falsely posturing in this way, the media news and talk shows should invite speakers who could bridge the gap with common sense proposals to help resolve the matter in a manner that could be bipartisan. Talk radio should do the same. It would take more work to identify such individuals, but bipartisanship is not yet totally out of the question.

Another possible way to generate more bipartisanship came up recently in the context of the horribly contentious Senate hearings to confirm Justice Kavanaugh. A simple majority is now required for confirmation of justices, not a supermajority as before. If a supermajority (60% or 67%) of House or Senate members were required for the passage of all bills, that requirement would force their members to pass more bipartisan legislation or risk losing re-election because they didn't manage to get anything done. Indeed, at least 14 state legislatures already have such supermajority requirements to pass bills that increase taxes.[28]

If the current divisiveness is not ameliorated, the grim alternative is to face the prospect of deterioration and decline which no one wants. We shouldn't want to wait for the next race riot to heed these words of a less-than-saintly Rodney

King appealing for calm during a 1992 race riot: "People, I just want to say, you know, can we all get along?"

Fortunately, bipartisanship may be dying, but it's not dead yet. In 2018 a bipartisan bill was passed and signed to address the opioid crisis. Criminal justice reform legislation in The First Step act was passed by the U.S. Senate by a vote of 87 to 12 on December 18, 2018, by the House on December 20 by a vote of 358 to 36, and signed into law by President Trump on December 21. Even with all sorts of other politically divisive issues swirling in Washington, including the longest government shutdown in history, our elected officials were still able to set aside their political posturing and put their heads together to work in a bipartisan fashion, if the issue was important enough for consensus to be reached. Let's all encourage more of this.

Now that the shutdown is over, it's time for both sides to come to the table, work out arrangements for border security, and compromise on some commonsense immigration policy. That's what the public wants and the country needs.

GET A FREE REVIEW COPY

IF YOU WANT TO REVIEW THIS BOOK OR FRACTURED AMERICA

Discover this powerful new book. It's all about crime, the police, criminal justice, and the opioid crisis.

Get a FREE review copy. Agree to review *Crime in America* or *Fractured America* and you'll get a FREE copy of a $14.95 paperback and $3.99 e-book.

Learn about our new books and win unique prizes!

You'll get a FREE copy of a $14.95 paperback and $3.99 e-book.

You'll also be the first to learn about our new books and have an opportunity to win unique prizes!

SEND ME MY REVIEW COPY
(www.crimeinamericapublishing.com)

ABOUT THE AUTHOR

Paul Brakke is a scientist based in the Little Rock, Arkansas area. He became interested in studying the criminal justice system because, as described in his first book *American Justice?*, his life was turned upside down by the system.

He has previously told his wife's story along with a critique of the criminal justice system in *American Justice?* After that, Brakke went on to look at other problems in the system and the country in general and how to fix them.

His other books include: *Crime in America, The Costly U.S. Prison System, Fixing the U.S. Criminal Justice System, Dealing with Illegal Immigration and the Opioid Crisis, The Price of Justice in America,* and *Cops Aren't Such Bad Guys.* To publish them, he set up a publishing company American Leadership Books, featuring books on criminal justice and social issues, which are available in print and e-books through Amazon, Ingram, Kindle, and other major distributors. Since these first books were directed primarily at law enforcement professionals, politicians, and academics, Brakke is now developing a series of books on criminal justice to appeal to the general public, especially to conservatives.

The books' website is: www.americanleadershipbooks.com.

Audiobooks are available at: https://www.audible.com/author/Paul-Brakke/B0714KG374

OTHER AVAILABLE BOOKS

Crime in America

Fixing the U.S. Criminal Justice System

The Price of Justice in America

The Costly U.S. Prison System

Cops Aren't Such Bad Guys

Dealing with Crime by Illegal Immigrants and the Opioid Crisis

CONTACT US

For more information:

        AMERICAN LEADERSHIP BOOKS
                8 Portia Drive
          Little Rock, Arkansas 72212
             brakkep@gmail.com

Notes

[1] Photo courtesy of Our Confederate Heroes: http://www.ourconfederateheros.org/wpcontent/uploads/2012/11/Major-Battles.jpg

[2] Jon Swaine, "Abraham Lincoln 'Wanted to Deport Slaves' to New Colonies," *The Telegraph,* February 11, 2011. http://www.telegraph.co.uk/news/worldnews/northamerica/usa/8319858/Abraham-Lincoln-wanted-to-deport-slaves-to-new-colonies.html

[3] Mark Mather, "U.S. Children in Single-Mother Families," Data Brief: PRB, May, 2010. http://www.prb.org/pdf10/single-motherfamilies.pdf

[4] Ana Gonzalez-Barrera and Jens Manuel Krogstad, "What we know about illegal immigration from Mexico", Pew Research Center, Factank, 12/3/2018. http://www.pewresearch.org/fact-tank/2018/12/03/what-we-know-about-illegal-immigration-from-mexico/

[5] Ibid.

[6] U.S. Customs and Border Protection, https://www.cbp.gov/newsroom/stats/sw-border-migration

[7] John Opdycke, "A 50 State Open Primary in 2020 Is Within Our Reach", *The Hill*; https://thehill.com/opinion/campaign/421399-a-50-state-open-primary-in-2020-is-within-our-reach

[8] Colin Woodard, *American Nations: A history of the eleven rival regional cultures in North America*, Viking, 2011.

[9] Helaine Olen, *The Washington Post,* "Age discrimination: a moral embarrassment", *Arkansas Democrat-Gazette*, 1/20/2019.

[10] John Rosemond, "Grandparents' age and wisdom no longer valued", *Arkansas Democrat-Gazette*, 1/22/2019.

[11] Chad Stone, Danilo Trisi, Arloc Sherman, and Roderick Taylor, "A Guide to Statistics on Historical Trends in Income Inequality", Center on Budget and Policy Priorities, updated 12/11/2018, https://www.cbpp.org/research/poverty-and-inequality/a-guide-to-statistics-on-historical-trends-in-income-inequality

[12] Tucker Carlson, *Ship of Fools. How a selfish ruling class is bringing America to the brink of revolution*, Free Press, New York, 2018, Introduction.

[13] Ibid., Chapter 1.

[14] Leon F. Selzer, "Greed: The Ultimate Addition," *Psychology Today*, October 17, 2012. https://www.psychologytoday.com/blog/evolution-the-self/201210/greed-the-ultimate-addiction

[15] Tim Dayton, "Money Addiction," *Huffington Post*, November 17, 2011. http://www.huffingtonpost.com/dr-tian-dayton/money-addiction_b_221937.html

[16] David John Marotta, "Dwight D. Eisenhower on Tax Cuts and a Balanced Budget," *Forbes,* February 28, 2013. https://www.forbes.com/sites/davidmarotta/2013/02/28/dwight-d-eisenhower-on-tax-cuts-and-a-balanced-budget/#7d4950115047

[17] Eric M. Johnson, "More than 500,000 people homeless in the United States: report", *Reuters*, 11/19/2015.

[18] Matthew Desmond, Evicted: *Poverty and Profit in the American City*, Crown Publishers, 2016.

[19] Eric M. Johnson, "More than 500,000 people homeless in the United States: report", *Reuters*, 11/19/2015.

[20] Emily Peiffer, "Why We Need to Stop Evictions Before They Happen", htpps://howhousingmatters.org/article/why-we-need-to-stop-evictions-before-they-happen/

[21] Matthew Desmond, *Evicted: Poverty and Profit in the American City*, Crown Publishers, 2016.

[22] Tyler Cohen, "Disappointing Economics," *Bloomberg News, Arkansas Democrat-Gazette*, 1/24/2019.

[23] Glenn Reynolds: "Civil War Has Already Begun In America", *USA Today*, 6/26/2018.

[24] Amy Gutmann and Dennis Thompson, *The Spirit of Compromise: Why Governing Demands It and Campaigning Undermines It*, Princeton University Press, 2012.

[25] Alan K. Simpson, back cover note on Amy Gutmann and Dennis Thompson, *The Spirit of Compromise: Why Governing Demands It and Campaigning Undermines It*, Princeton University Press, 2012.

[26] Amy Gutmann and Dennis Thompson, *The Spirit of Compromise*, Princeton University Press, 2012.

[27] Carl Hulse, Chamber of Commerce Decides Bipartisanship is Good Business", *NY Times*, 2/3/2019.

[28] Liz Farmer, "Raising Taxes Could Be Harder Now in Florida", Governing, 11/7/2018. http://www.governing.com/topics/finance/gov-florida-supermajorities-tax-ballot.html

www.ingramcontent.com/pod-product-compliance
Lightning Source LLC
Chambersburg PA
CBHW050204130526
44591CB00034B/2084